# Chats in the Woods
Written by Angie Owens Bennett

**Note to storyteller:** Chats in the Woods is written to be read aloud. The sounds of the animals are written phonetically. The natural lilt of your voice will approximate the animal's call. Don't worry about whether or not you say it right, just have fun with your kids.

This book is dedicated to my Dad, Gene Owens.
Thanks for all the walks in the woods and all the bedtime stories you made up on the spot for me.

Every day in the woods, animals
chat . . .

Birds sing . . .

Frogs croak . . .

And insects chirp the seconds and minutes by.

They work finding nuts, seeds,
berries and . . .

**Fish** to eat.

They build homes.

They care for their young.

In the morning, Dove's little ones
wake up crying:
**Ooh-wah-hoo-oo-oo**

Robin's family cheers them up:
**Cheerily Cheriup Cherio Cheerily**

To start the day, everyone washes up.

Barred Owl asks:

**Who-cooks-for-you?**

**Who-cooks-for-you-all?**

Quail answers:  **Bob-White!**

Carolina Wren boils a pot of tea. When it is ready, she calls the other animals with a whistle: **Tea-kettle! Tea-kettle! Tea-kettle!**

Down at the pond, the turtle family
climbs out of the water to listen to. . .

Wood Thrush.  She lets out a yodel:
**ee-oh-lay-o-wee.**

In the evening, when the sun sets over
the pond and woods, geese fly home
to their nests. Honk!-Honk!

Toads begin their evening lullaby trill.

Green Frogs gulp:
**Goonk!-Gunk!-Gunk!**

Bullfrogs croak a rhythm:
**Jug-a-rum . . .Jug-a-rum . . .
Jug-a-rum**.

Fireflies light the way home
for the animals.

Mothers kiss their young goodnight before . . .

They snuggle down in their warm, cozy beds and fall asleep because they are very  tired.

You're looking very sleepy, too.
Maybe you should go to bed.

Goodnight, Sweetheart.